Still Here

A POETRY MEMOIR OF GRIEF & LOVE

JENNY SMITH

FOREWORD BY
REV. LARA BOLGER

Praise for Still Here

Each one of these poems is a little scalpel. They tenderly cut through the layers of social padding we like to keep around death and grief.

Jenny's crisp, clear language brings us into direct contact with the wildness of loss. And as we follow her through her experience we get closer to—and more compassionate with—our own.

James. A Pearson, Poet & Author

In both love and loss, one recognizes the true voice of a kindred soul. There are no greater times when an authentic voice is needed, and in "Still Here", Jenny Smith, invites us into personal, thoughtful moments; not as observers, but those gathered into the same room. We are taken on a journey through private moments of grief and love. In a style reminiscent of Luci Shaw, Smith's beautifully crafted words of simple verse hang on the page and you find yourself reaching for them, returning again and again, as if holding them in your hand. These poems will give you something to hold on to and remember for as often as you need them.

Ray Buckley, Author & Storyteller

Jenny Smith has written a grief book that takes us both to the depths of pain and loss and gives us the grace to keep living. Her poems offer profoundly important permissions to the bereaved. Her poems chronicle vivid moments in the aftermath of a sudden death, like the sweater she wore in the hospital, putting on mascara again, and crying in the cheese aisle at the grocery store. Throughout the collection, the author watches herself without judgment as she learns to face her loss. Her willingness to observe the changes in herself gives grieving readers the gift of solidarity as they navigate becoming people who have stories of loss. Jenny reminds us we're all grieving something. In the form of a book of poems, she has given us the space we need to be honest about our losses and the courage we dream of to keep living anyway.

Rev. Katy Shedlock
Pastor, Slam Poet & Community Organizer

Jenny Smith has given us a piece of herself. *Still Here* is an honest collection of poetry that invites each reader to be seen as it invites you to hold grief and joy, sorrow and hope. This book is a personal invitation to lean into the hurt and hope of living. Jenny puts into words the depth of our emotions as we wrestle with and the emotions we feel. Like a trusted friend, she offers us something vulnerable and brave.

Tanner Olson
Author, Poet & Speaker

Deeply personal and raw. Deeply profound and relatable. Jenny Smith's grief poetry collection "Still Here" is an incredibly beautiful and moving book of poems.

Crafted with care, the author reaches into the depths of her grieving heart to share the realities of immense loss. Her words bear witness to the painful realities of death while bravely exploring the truth that love still remains and persists. This book will resonate so deeply with grieving hearts. The poems will make the reader feel validated in their emotional process and encouraged to journey through their grief gently with arms and hearts open to the light and hope that can still be found there. I cannot recommend this book enough. Well done.

Liz Newman, author of *I Look To The Mourning Sky: A Book of Poems and Writing Prompts for the Grieving Heart*

For many loss and journeying through grief is a difficult process because it is seen as something to avoid, push away, or blame someone else for the pain we might be experiencing. Jenny takes us through the raw pain of loss letting the reader see the on-going process of integration of those memories triggered by day-to-day experiences giving the person the opportunity to pay attention to the intense feelings, emotions, seeing them as opportunities to learn about themself so that they might live life more fully, more deeply and more full of grace.

Rev. Dr. Judy Jewell, United Methodist Retired Pastor & Bereavement Specialist

Having recently lost dear loved ones, my inner being was almost numb. This book invited me to dialogue and dance gently with loss, grief, and death. A dance that helps me move towards a new rhythm of gratefulness for departed loved ones, our memories together, and my own life as it is today. Thank you, Jenny Smith.

Rev. David Valera, Executive Director of Connectional Ministries of the Pacific Northwest Conference

Jenny Smith's collection of poems, *Still Here,* isn't a glossy memory book of a beloved brother but an intimate and quietly heart-breaking ode to the ways that love lives long beyond the boundaries of time and skin that carry it.

For those of us who have lost a beloved to death... you will see yourself here, in the depths, the darknesses, the wanderings, and the gratitudes. And for those of us who have walked and watched as another grieved, hard to reach but in so much need... here, too, you'll find the tensile strength and tenderness of the connective tissues amongst us all. A common humanity in which we all know at the soul level what Jenny means when she writes, *'i did not expect a/ quiet monday/ to be the worst day yet.'*

Whether you read it as a travelogue through the early days of another's grief or as a poem-by-poem reminder that you are not alone in your own loss, *Still Here* will bring you gifts beyond measure.

Rev. Julia Nielsen, Deacon of Sacred Organizing, Leaven Community Land & Housing Coalition

Jenny Smith's poetry memoir Still Here is powerful and life-giving, even as she writes of death. The raw honesty with which she speaks is gift and grace in a culture that does not talk about grief and loss. In allowing us—through these poems—to accompany her as she journeys "through the valley of the shadow of death," she gives us permission to acknowledge and name our own griefs and losses, and to make our way through them in our own time, and in our own way.

Her words remind us that we are not alone; that life—including grief, which is part of life—is both/and, that it all "dances together here in this moment" and that love does not end with loss. It can and does grow, and grow stronger. As someone who has dealt with sudden, unexpected loss, in *Still Here*, I found truth and authenticity, and life and hope.

Kathy Swaar, MA, author of *Fine Lines: Walking the Labyrinth of Grief and Loss*

Still Here: A Poetry Memoir of Grief and Love offers a kindness and hospitality to those whose hearts have been shredded by the loss of someone they hold dear. Only we can grieve the way we must, yet Jenny's words become a companion on our lonely way. Her intimacy with fresh grief washes the pages with an honest account of how lament will have its own way and how grief can draw us deeper into Love to find solace and hope.

Charlotte Ferris, Spiritual director, pilgrimage leader and founder of Wild Edge of Faith

There is something about grief that invites us into the in-between spaces of our lives – the heavy pauses in the midst of weeping, the silence between breaths that never seems deep enough, the blank gaze we find ourselves offering into a world that feels as if it is shaking us to our very core.

In this book of heart-wrenching and life-affirming poetry, Jenny Smith honors these in-between spaces and gifts us with a raw and real look into the heart of grief. For all who have experienced the intimate piercing of such a moment – the loss of a loved one, of a dream, of an identity once held to be true – this collection of poems serves as a worthy companion along the path toward healing.

> Andy Lang, author of *Unmasking the Inner Critic: Lessons for Living an Unconstricted Life*

Tears streamed down my face as Jenny's words gently and honestly walked me into the complex emotional and unpredictable journey of her own grief. To echo the words of Howard Thurman, I heard the "sound of the genuine" awakening in me, allowing me the courage to walk with her into the caverns of grief I carry inside. Her voice invites us to be brave enough to face the heartbreaking reality of our lives with the honesty and love that ultimately brings about healing. This is a part of the human journey all of us desperately need to take in this moment in time, and I'm so glad her words are out there in the world to be a companion for us as we do.

> Rev. April Blaine, Lead Pastor, Hilliard United Methodist Church, Adjunct Professor of Spirituality, Methodist Theological School in Ohio

contents

PART TWO
EVERY DAY GRIEF

Dad, Mom, Ryan & Lauren —

I still don't understand us without him.
May these poems be a whisper of the love he so generously gave us.
It's the honor of a lifetime to love him alongside each of you.
Still.

To my brilliant artists & illustrators —

*You stepped into these poems and brought them to life. Your love
for Jeremy shimmers in these pages.
Thank you.*

*Isabella Smith
Wesley Smith
Aaron Smith
Kim Beckett
Dave Beckett
Lauren Keller
Camden Keller
Kylie Keller
Becky Becker
Emily Evans
Emily Goodrum
Marah Lambert
Andria Queen*

foreword

My life has overlapped with Jenny Smith's in many ways over the years. We are both United Methodist pastors who served on the same regional committee, ministered in the same district, and participated in the same continuing education workshops for the past seven years.

After collaborating with her on a seminar for a clergy gathering, I started following her Palms Up approach. I subscribed to her bi-monthly emails, in which she shared her experience of living a more present, grounded, and sacred life. Jenny's honest and vulnerable sharing touched me deeply and enlivened my Spirit. I eventually signed up for a small group experience she facilitated with five other women who were also seeking a deeper, contemplative experience. Jenny's gift of holding space for honest sharing reassured me that I was in a place I could truly be myself. More than my valued colleague, Jenny became what Celtic Christianity calls an *anamcara*: a soul friend.

On Wednesday, February 16, 2022, I met Jenny for coffee in Marysville, WA. I knew we would be pouring out our hearts to each other, because our lives had overlapped yet again: we were both two weeks into a one-year break from full time pastoral ministry. We were both facing thresholds and transitions in our personal and professional lives that felt significant. But neither of us knew what was on the horizon.

Two days later, while Jenny was on a much-anticipated couples' vacation in San Diego, her beloved youngest brother, Jeremy, suffered a fatal aneurism due to an arteriovenous malformation (AVF) in his brain. Our worlds were now inextricably bound together in a new way, this time by the twin threads of grief and loss.

I was grieving the untimely death of my father just nine months previously. Over coffee, I shared with Jenny that I was looking forward to going to California to be with my family for the one-year anniversary of his death, but I didn't fully know the profound ways that my grief could reshape my life.

As pastors, both Jenny and I were trained about the grieving process: how to honor it, make space for it, and normalize it. Yet, when grief was now in the driver's seat of my own life, nothing seemed normal. I was afraid that grief would have its own way, if I really let it in – so I pushed grief away. I became an expert at keeping grief at arm's length.

Now Jenny was in the same car as me, and we were both grief's passengers.

What happened next was an unexpected grace. Jenny started posting a few of her poems. Every time I read them; my heart flung open. She was able to give grief a voice – a much needed, truthful voice. Her words, as you will experience, are relatable, raw, tender, and heart-wrenching. Her ability to be real and honest unlocks the healing aspects of grief; and her experience reveals a beautiful wisdom. By being present to the moment, no matter how uncomfortable, and being willing to write it down, she uncovers the places where pain and joy meet, and where love lives. Like all good poets, the more personal one gets with their experience, the more universal the truth. I found myself reading and re-reading these profound truths of love and transcendence, participating in her process of integrating Jeremy's life and love with hers.

Jenny is a gentle guide on the road of grief and healing. Reading her words gave me permission to go deeper into my own grief, with all its contradictions and confusing feelings. I see her poems as entry points, doorways, invitations, that you can enter and connect with wherever you are in your journey. May you discover the wisdom of your grief and the love that bears it through my dear friend Jenny's poetry. I believe that is exactly what her brother hopes will happen too. He's *still here.*

Rev. Lara Bolger

introduction

I wish I could write you a book filled with words that tell you exactly how to grieve and love. Lose and heal. But I imagine that would be a boring book because no one likes a know-it-all. Even when we crave certainty and direction when life falls apart, aren't we mostly looking for solidarity? A sense that we're not the only one. That others have walked this path. That this pain won't kill us. That there's freedom in realizing there's no right way to walk this road. That a love bigger than us holds us while we stumble forward.

Those were the things I searched for when life fell apart. This book is what I needed in the early months of grief when my brain had zero capacity to read more than a paragraph at a time. These poems are brief and to the point. Each one attempts to articulate the chaos of grief in a moment of pain and reflection. I wrote them on my phone in parking lots, by hospital beds, on morning walks, while crying in bed, while waiting in the school pick up line, or making dinner.

While grief is never linear, it is worth a note that the poems you're about to engage are written in a linear timeline. Within hours of the phone call, I started tapping out poems and notes in my phone. We journey deep into shock, the daily-ness of grief, and the first sparks of wanting to live again.

The illustrations are created by family and friends' of my brother. I hope their immense love for him deepens the words on the page for you.

At the end you'll find the story of my brother's passing. I share the words written for his funeral and blessings for members of our family in the first month. My brother donated many of his organs and we navigated that process with gratitude and sadness. I include a note to a recipient and a couple responses. My son wrote a poem and my daughter drew you a picture.

These poems demand nothing from you. They are an offering from my broken heart to yours, trusting these grief journeys pour us into deeper love and grace. You're welcome to read them in order or flip open any page at any time. It's okay if you read one and then this book sits on your shelf for five months or five years and then you pick it up again.

While my brain still strains for a clearly defined healing pattern, grief refuses to cooperate. I shift from anger to shock to acceptance to rage in a matter of hours. Much love if that's your story too. Grief has a mind of its own.

————

Grief will wreck a life in the best way possible, if we let it. I hate silver lining grief, but the truth remains: I'm a more honest human because my brother died. I'm uncovering and healing painful parts of my story because I get how short life is now. I use far more tissues to wipe sad eyes but I'm more in touch with my emotions than ever before. When people in my life experience fresh loss, I mark my calendar to check in with them periodically instead of assuming they're fine. I'm learning more about love than I would have expected.

Beloved reader, may grace hold you as you sit with this

body of work. May words and images resound with the ache of grief that rests in your body. May these stories move you wherever you need to go next. May a deep sense of rest settle in your soul.

Grief really is this terrible.

And.

We will be okay.

PART ONE

shock

words on airplanes

i'm anxious to see you
i'm scared
i hate hospitals

but i love you

so i will walk in those doors
i will sit by you
i will hold your hand
i will cry

i will say goodbye

but i don't want to

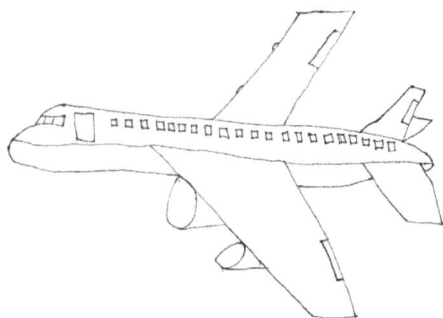

change of address

they say my brother will die today
but he's already gone

his spirit is home

i want his spirit with us
here
now
his humanity
his humor
his love

just one more text
one more call
one more hug

sweet brother
i know you're safe
free
loved

but we miss you

this can't be real

complex invitations

every part of this is both/and

grief doesn't cancel love
sadness doesn't cancel gratitude
worry doesn't cancel memories
death doesn't cancel life

it all dances together
here in this moment

i just hate that i got invited

joy jumping

our beloved died a week ago

on saturday we stood
in front of a bouncy house
at his memorial service
and took our first family photo
with him in a frame
instead of standing with us

someone may glance at that
and think *they must be so strong*

it doesn't feel like strength
it's been the worst week of our lives

it feels like despair
that's fighting for hope

it feels like shock

it feels like love

pounding heart

all i want
is for people
to see
how much
it hurts
so they can
know how much
love there was

tell me this matters
our relationship
his life
my pain
our love
our family

tell me it matters

you bearing witness
reminds my broken
heart this pain
won't kill me

ten years old

sweet girl
i sense your heaviness
the frantic worry that
somehow you failed
your little brother

that if you somehow knew —
you could have saved him

i hear you
i feel you
i see you

may i set you free
from this terrible burden

you loved your brother
the best you knew how
he knew it too

there's nothing you could have done
sweet girl

nothing

it's okay to unclench your hands
from your heart

let it breathe
let it receive
let it live

trusting that your love for him
was enough

that this love will sustain you for a lifetime
of learning to live without his hugs
his smile
his laughter
his care

sweet girl
he's with you
listen closely
he's everywhere

take heart
this brother you cared for
will now care for you
with love
and joy
and adventure
and grace

it's okay to let go
you did nothing wrong

proposals + funerals

we can access
love and grace
absolutely
anywhere
anytime

and

it's nice to have
spaces that
so consistently
feel safe and
full of love

i've been playing
piano in the sanctuary
at this church in alaska
since i was 16

today i sat my 39-year-old
self down on that bench
and filled the room with music

i discerned a call to
ministry in this room

i watched my dad
lead worship in this room

i preached my first sermon
in this room

my husband proposed
to me in this room

my kids learned
to crawl in this room

i held my mom's hand
as we sang in this room

i served as a pastor
in this room

and now we said
goodbye to my brother
in this room

i hate adding this to the list

that's life isn't it?

the love and the pain
the joy and the heartbreak
the laughter and the tears

we can't get one
without the other

grieving with new friends

i need hugs
from people
who knew me
when he was alive

boycotting hygiene

two weeks of tears
dry on my face
gently flaking off
as i touch my cheeks

evidence of deep love
and deep pain

i don't want to
wash my face

i'll wash away
one more connection
to the one i lost

one last glance

it's my last time in your house
i don't want to leave
i don't want to move forward without you
i'm sitting on your bed looking around

your cat's ashes
your fake fireplace
your surprisingly clean bathroom
your beautiful view
your favorite artwork
your wrinkled clothes on the floor
a book i wrote in your drawer
pictures my kids drew you

i feel close to you here
the place you slept
the space you laughed

and

you're going with me
into all my unknowns
all my adventures

i want to live my life
like really live
i want to travel and see beautiful things
i want to love people like you did
i want to share you with others

please go with me

i'm standing to leave this room
not because i'm ready
or because i want to
but because i know
you go with me
and i'm choosing
to believe this isn't
goodbye

grief bubbles

i don't want to leave alaska
i don't want to leave the spot
where you were last conscious

i don't want to leave your dog
i don't want to leave our brother's home
and the spot on the couch
i've inhabited for three weeks

i don't want to leave the mountains
i don't want to leave this church family
i don't want to leave your car
parked in the driveway

i don't want to leave your friends
i don't want to leave our mom and brother
i don't want to leave all the
physical reminders of you
i don't want to leave the snow
that's crunched under my feet
for three weeks

this bubble
while terrible and heartbreaking
felt safe

inside the bubble
we could pretend you were
about to run up the stairs to say hi

inside the bubble
most everyone knew you

there was so much
we didn't have to say

inside the bubble
we knew our rhythms of grief
and living in this strange new reality

i first felt the trepidation
of growing the bubble
when we walked into the
two public gatherings to honor your life

a part of me didn't want to
share you with anyone else
this was our grief
our loss

but then — i saw again
how powerful love and community are

the bigger bubble didn't erase you
it amplified your love

we felt carried along
on a tidal wave of care and love

but now i leave the alaska bubble
no one really knows you
if they do — they didn't *know* you

maybe the bigger bubble
will feel good too
but it doesn't feel that way now

so i choose to trust things

i know are true
even if i don't feel it yet

you go with me
your love and story go with me
life continues
one foot in front of the other

ready or not
here we go

one step

my heart screams at me
to stop taking
that step forward

to root my feet
to the spot where
life changed

as if i can delay
the horrific absurdity
of this new reality

yet

feet are made for walking
for taking kids to school
running errands
making dinner

so if one must
take a step forward
may that step be gentle
purposeful
full of love and grace
for all this hurting heart holds

all of it

grief is not either/or

it's not crying in my
morning eggs or smiling

it's not looking at old pictures
or dreaming about the future

it's not holding a hat he loved
or making dinner plans for next week

it's not processing complicated anger
or taking kids to the park on a sunny day

it's not checking in with family
or finding brain capacity for normal life tasks

it's not his life or mine

there are moments where
i forget that he died
i hate those moments
the remembering is the worst

it makes me want to
set up camp inside the sadness
to build some walls
so i can keep the happiness out

the happiness feels too happy

and yet

it's both/and

yes to body-shaking tears
yes to memories that ache
yes to the grief of plans cut short
yes to denial, shock and disbelief
yes to a sunny spring day
yes to cousins' laughter
yes to making plans for the summer
yes to allowing happiness to exist in my body

it's not happy or sad
it's allowing both to be true
whenever they rise

traveling grief

we took you to oregon this weekend

we packed up our bags for a last minute trip
to see family because it feels good to be
with people who knew you

i gently placed your framed photo on the
top of our suitcase and zipped it up

you hung out on the counter
in my sister's house all weekend
you watched our movie
heard the kids laughing
noticed the tears during
late night conversations
heard the banter from adults
who genuinely enjoy being together

then when it was time for hugs and goodbyes
i picked you up off the counter and
handed you to dad
would you be willing to hold
him for our family picture?
he nodded

we took the photo
a mix of kids' antics and smiles
with heavy stories hidden inside

i placed your photo back
in my bag and we drove back home
i gently set you back on your

photo ledge in our kitchen
so i can see you everyday

it feels good to imagine you
still a part of our family rituals
the gaping hole is painfully obvious
and heartbreaking to feel over and over
i can't imagine simply erasing you
from the story
you go with us still

here's to all the ways we grieve
the creative ways we include a beloved
the ways their spirit lives on in us
knowing everyone needs something different

and for the utter pain that
we'd rather have their living
breathing body any day
than some framed picture in a bag

quiet mondays

i expected the middle
of the night phone call
to break my heart

i expected the hospital
to be terrible

i expected the funeral
to be gut wrenching

i expected the first days
to be hell

i did not expect a
quiet monday
to be the worst day yet

i choose not to resist or fight it

i open my hands to notice
to allow it
to let it be

stuck

i'd rather hide in my tears
than move forward without you

hiding

the unwanted home
i've carved out
with a title scrawled
over the door
— grief

is quickly becoming
an oddly comforting home

some days
i never want to leave

what first felt
violent and vicious
now feels
comforting and familiar

so much so that
normal life now feels
violent and vicious

i'd like to hide out here
as long as possible

surrounded by tears
and pictures
and memories

i'm told i will
integrate it all
and take my beloved
with me

when i step outside

but i'm not there yet

i much prefer this
cozy little terrible
home of grief

thank you for
knocking on the door
once in a while
to remind me
you're still here

even as i resist
stepping outside
into the light

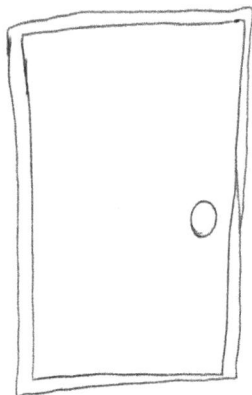

grace + shock

my therapist said
you'll be in shock
for two to four months
then you'll start to thaw

it will hurt in a different way

i'm so grateful for shock

for the cushion in
these early months

shock enabled me to
pick up my phone
and book flights to alaska
within minutes of getting the news

shock enabled me to
string words together
and tell our world the worst news

shock enabled me to
laugh at a ted lasso episode
while eating good food
and snuggling with his dog

shock enabled me to
sort through his closet
so someone could make
pillows out of his favorite shirts

shock enabled me to

pack my kids' lunches
and give them a sense of routine
when i wanted to stay in bed and cry

the thaw creeps in once in a while
it hurts differently
it's sharper
more final

it feels more like
what the hell just happened?!
which always feels a little weird
after just traveling
this road for a month

shock, thank you for protecting us

for ever so slowly allowing us
to see more layers of this pain
when we're able to see them

the waking up is painful
no matter when it happens
but at least shock softens the blow
with a little bit of grace

the worst game

i play a terrible game with my brain

it's been four weeks since he died
every little bit or so
i force myself to remember it's real
i hold my breath to see
what my brain will do this time

sometimes i know it's true
i nod to the truth
and keep going

sometimes i'm shocked all over again
tears sting my eyes
my throat grows tight with pain
i double over with the terror of a sister
who lost her baby brother

sometimes i smile
because i know he's okay
and i will be too

i can't tell yet if it's a cruel game
or the daily work of grief

either way
it hurts
and
it feels
like healing

silence

i hear his voice
when i watch old videos

i cannot imagine
our family
without his voice

our goodbye

i watched a tv show today
where two siblings said goodbye
as one moved away

my eyes flooded with emotion
remembering all over again that
i never got that goodbye
with my brother before he died

we talked on a thursday night
and he was gone 24 hours later

my heart wandered as i imagined
how that conversation might have gone

if we somehow knew
he would die that evening
i'd have looked him in the eyes
and told him all the ways he mattered to me
to so many people
that the way he loved us changed us
that the way he laughed
helped us set down the heaviness
that the way he saw the world
felt like love
that the way he encouraged us
made us think we could fly

i'd lean in and say
all those beautiful things aside
he would have rolled his eyes and smirked
what i need you to most know

is that i'm so damn grateful
i got to love you
and that i will spend the rest of my life
loving people the way
you loved me

i would have given him the longest biggest hug
knowing that 33 years of stories, love, and trust
flowed between us

i would have never left that hug
i would have tried to stop
all that was about to unfold

he would have glanced back
over his shoulder
winked and said
palms up, right?

i'd have punched him in the arm
and laughed through the
glistening tears in my eyes

yeah brother
palms up

awkward

part of me feels like
i should stop talking
about grief so much

i imagine thumbs scrolling by
and rolling eyes
geez — we get it
you're sad

shame simmers
before it burns off
and i see what's
actually true

grief is
awkward
annoying
uncomfortable
tempting to ignore

but then
i remember
another reason
i'm willing to
show up
writing about
something most of us
intensely dislike

we're all grieving something

all

of
us

the pandemic
job loss
change in relationships
parenting challenges
systems that harm
with no accountability
loss of a beloved
a change in a physical ability
a tough diagnosis
aging

grief is a part of living
no matter how good
we think we are at
pushing it away

i promise to keep showing up
to whatever is in front of me
knowing a few words here
and there may help you
show up to whatever is in front of you

we really are in this together

keyboard nightmares

my finger hovers
over my keyboard
not wanting to click
publish

we have final word
that our brother
officially died
this afternoon

it was time
to hit publish

i hesitate
as if not pressing
that button
makes this just a
terrible dream

my family gently
nods
it's time

i click publish
and burst into tears

oh to return to a life
before having to share
news like that

fabric memories

the nurse complimented
my sweater as i walked
into icu to say goodbye to you

how could she think
about sweaters
at a time like this

i offered a weak smile
and nodded

i wore that sweater
every day for a month

maybe this will work

there's a moment
where i think
all the meaning making
will bring them back

the pillow made of their clothes
the tattoo with their fingerprint
the glass pendant with their ashes
the framed collage on the wall
the poems and stories told
the necklace they held in their bed

i know it's how we remember
honor
grieve
heal

and yet

i do each one .
hoping this time
they'll magically
appear

grief tricks

there's a piercing moment between
denial and stinging tears

a split second when i think
i can choose
to believe you died
or pretend it's a nightmare

the story ends the same way
every time

but for a piercing moment
i think i have a choice

love bravely

when we speak of our beloved we miss
we're not spreading grief
burying ourselves in the depths of loss
throwing a wet blanket on the
party of denial we all love

what if we're spreading love
refusing to erase the gifts we received
clinging to the story that changed us
the love that gave us life

could we be people who spread love
at the very moment our world
tells us to shrink back
and recoil at the discomfort of grief

what if the desire
to name your grief
is the gift of love
others need

speak their name
tell their story
tell your story

it might be the thing
that wakes us up
from our terrible denial
that we'll escape the story of loss

ready

if i'm being honest
i'm waiting for
sustained moments
of acceptance that
he died
before i take
big steps forward

i know it doesn't
work like that
but each time
i crumble
i don't feel ready

may i be willing
even when i don't
feel ready

still in my phone

something really great happened today
i called each family member to celebrate
until i got to your number
and burst into tears

operation hide

i wear sunglasses everywhere
because i never know when
tears will roll

temptation

don't do it
my brain screams
it hurts too much

i press play on a
video of my brother

my chest fills
with a sharp inhale

how is he gone?

echo

you're gone
you're gone
you're gone

i echo the refrain
trying to teach my brain
the truth

yet
remembering
hurts the most

an empty line

some nights i lie awake
thinking about our goodbye
your hospital bed
and me shaking with fear
as i tried to say
goodbye
to you

no idea how to
honor thirty-three years
together with a few minutes
of one-sided conversation

hating the anxiety that
shook my body
fearful i would dissolve
at my next sharp breath

i absolutely hated
our goodbye

even though i'm told
it's rare we even got that
after what you experienced

still

i would give the world
to have gotten
one last conversation

the kind where

a soft smile
and a nod
said everything
we needed
to say

the corner of lake otis + willene

today i stood in your tire tracks
the last place your eyes
looked at this land you've loved
since you were three

i wonder what you felt
what you thought
what moved through
your soul as life
crumbled

did you think of what
was left undone
or unsaid
or unloved

did some part of you
breathe deeply of it all
with gratitude and peace

because you knew something
so many don't

this life is a gift
and you lived it as such

today i stood in your tracks
soaking the melting snow
with my tears
anger
pain
sorrow

and i felt your love
like a light breeze
surround my ache

once again loving me
back to life

PART TWO

every day grief

bless

shock — i feel you wearing off

you were beautiful gift
in these early weeks
wrapped around
the jagged edges
of sheer terror

i'm grateful for you
how you cushioned the panic
blessed the pain
offered respite in between
the waves

shock — i bless you

some days
i wish you'd return

i know i'll survive
but facing this pain
without you
feels unsurvivable

let them fall

i see you
having a moment of sadness
that feels as if it will never end

a human enters your bubble of grief
and you reach to wipe away your tears
as if your sadness will offend
frighten
disrupt
the heart of this intruder

we lament the generations
of conditioning that hiss
and shame you into reaching
for your cheek

what if we did this differently

what if you didn't brush
away your tears

what if they continued to roll
telling the story of love lost
presence denied
a breaking heart

what if the tears
we didn't wipe away
served our own healing
and the healing of the one
who bears witness

maybe we all need to learn
how to sit with one
who doesn't brush away the tears

calendars

life is moving forward
and i hate it

you should be here
at the family gatherings
making new memories
laughing and joking
smiling and making plans

you should be a call away
a text or funny meme
at the ready

you should call me this weekend
to catch up
to share what's difficult
how you're really doing

and i would listen
really
listen
because i would never
take it for granted again

life is moving forward and
i hate a world without you

everything familiar
feels awkward now

getting groceries
taking the kids to school

walking the neighborhood
turning the calendar page
seeing your name in my phone

life is moving forward
and i hate it

numb

sometimes i summon a cry
to wake my heart from
the numbing slumber
because you feel closer
when the tears roll

gentle love

i can either beat
this grief into submission
or hold it so gently
that she feels safe
to keep showing up
whenever she wants
to be witnessed

lunch plans

sometimes i think
i'll heal the grief
if i excavate every last tear
from my body

then i'm surprised
when one tiny wobbly
step forward
heals

mascara

i put on my makeup
for the first time in months
as if i could force a new story
to be true

a story where you
still get to live

or

maybe its a story
where i
still
get
to
live

lemonade

the sun hangs in the sky
longer than it did
when you died

sandals and shorts
lemonade and porch swings
grace my days

you feel farther
and farther
away

breeze

somehow that leaf
fluttering in the wind
is a love poem
from the one
i still can't believe
is gone

grief time

dissolving into grief time
is equal parts
terrible
and holy

life moves along
with what starts to feel
normal

then a memory falls into my lap
and i choose to either
swallow the grief
or welcome it

sunset

tonight i laid in bed
and watched the sun
fall from the sky

i ignored the dishes
the paperwork
the tv
even my family

because i missed you

dance of the living

dancing in the kitchen
brings this grieving body
to life

the music meets the ache
with love
with possibility
with a deep breath

the beat pulses
like the rhythm of my beloved
who dances now in the breeze
the flutter of a leaf
the bird on the back porch

as our souls heal and move
we give each other a nod

it's okay to keep living

to the ones who've lost

i never knew
the unspeakable pain
you held
for the one you lost

the pain people dismissed
forgot
denied

i wish i'd known
what to say then

i think i do now

first family gathering

gathering in the place
you've always been
hurts so much

yet i look
at these people
who love you
and i see them
choose courage
every time

every hug
tear
joke
hug

feels like courage
hope
honesty

they never deny the pain
it hung out with us
all weekend

and

we laugh
we dance in a talent show
we tell new stories
we remember old ones
we talk about you
we plan new trips

it is pure courage
imagining a new world
where we hurt
and
we still live

day 72

the shock is thawing

somehow it hurts more now
than it did then

life moves forward
calendars fill up again
bodies relax into laughter
smiles seem more real

and yet

forward movement
can never erase a story
that lives in a grieving body

how can this life be
if they aren't here

we do what we can
we love our bodies as they ache
we clear calendars when we need quiet
we set down busyness so we can feel
we nod to their presence and smile
we hold the ache so gently
that tears flow and heal

sad fog

i glanced at your picture
on the shelf today

a deep sigh settled
in my spirit
like early morning fog
on a mountain lake

i *still* cannot imagine
a world that exists
without your essence
your secret sauce
your heart
your laugh

the fog clears
once in a while
and gratitude sings

but mostly
the fog is
heavy
and
grief-stricken

half cup

you'll get about
a half cup of your brother
i hear my mom say

ashes — my sister reminds me
we're talking about ashes

we crack jokes
and choke back tears
to smooth the absurdity
and the horror
of a conversation
about our
beloved's
body

tattoo

i got my first tattoo today
it only hurt a little

sister's smile and
brother's joy
made me feel brave

watching an artist
etch your fingerprint
onto my arm
made you somehow feel
closer

and
actually
gone

you weren't there

we celebrated mother's day
this weekend
but you weren't there

well

your body wasn't there
your laughter wasn't there
your naps on the couch didn't happen
the kids missed playing with you
we missed you at the dinner table
we missed you in our late night conversations

we missed you so much it hurt
and yet

your love was there

when the kids sang sanctuary at the talent show
when the guys danced to shake it off
when we watched basketball
when we played by the river
when we sang happy birthday
when we drank your beer
when your brother spent hours with the kids
when we cried because we missed you
when we ate chip dip and crescent rolls
when we got tattoos for you
when we painted rocks with things you love
when isabella wrapped a gift like you would
when we threw puffy balls over the balcony
when i read a poem and tears fell

when we talked about what really matters
when we hugged extra hard
when we said i love you way more than usual

your love is here
even if you're not

no reason

my body is sad today
i used to need a reason

now i just make space for
her to feel sad

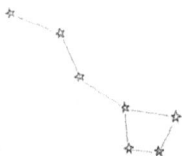

tornado

it seems particularly cruel
that losing a beloved
also upsets the balance
of every single part of your life

as if losing them wasn't
enough

okay

three months ago
the phone rang
the prognosis was not good

my shell-shocked self
told my brother
5287 miles away
whatever happens
it will be okay again

in those early moments
i scrambled for solid ground
as the earth shook beneath us

three months later
i look at your picture
and know all over again

somehow
it will be okay again
and
nothing
is okay

sleeping love

you hugged me
last night
in a dream

we talked
but i don't
much remember
what we said

all i remember
is how it
felt
to hug you
again

that was real

for sale signs

your house went on
the market today

i cried in the
grocery store line
when i saw the link

your kitchen
your room
your view
your home

now someone new
will call it theirs

i hope they feel
deeply loved
in that space

i know you'd want that

but i still wish
you lived there

two ounces

a wave hits
while cleaning
on saturday

i pick up
a small
medicine bottle
that holds
your ashes

who knew
an entire life
could end up
in a two ounce
container

empty

i keep waiting for you
to walk through the door
in this place
you've always been

my mind plays tricks
on my heart
each time
the door opens

but you never
walk through

love

some days i cry
because i'm
so damn grateful
i got to love you

and be
loved
by
you

ready or not

the one i miss
more than life
told me it was okay
to keep living

i believe him

we always love
People, even
when we
can't see
them

they get it

i pulled up my sleeve
and showed your
fingerprint to
three new
friends
today

tears shimmered
in their understanding
eyes

they knew the pain
i knew

your life has a way
of connecting me
to new souls
with astonishing
grace

grief heals

i love that our family
is growing closer
and doing the
terribly good work
of grief

i hate that
you're gone
and don't get
to enjoy this

anniversary dresses

windows down
music on
tears and sunlight streaming
smile on my face

your essence inhabits
every square inch
of this perfection

how is it that
you are so present
in every moment
of my joy
just like you're
present in every moment
of my heart-breaking grief?

i welcome the tears
as i sit in the parking lot
preparing to get a dress
for my wedding anniversary

whiplash

everything in my body
used to pull me forward
to the future
to possibilities
to new memories

now everything
in my body
pulls me back
to when you
were alive

i don't want to grow
because each step
of growth takes me
farther away from you

even though
i know its
not true

which is it?

i built a cozy little bubble
where my grief was normal
my anger was understood
my sadness was welcomed
my silence was comfortable
my trauma was soothed
my belovedness was acknowledged

some days i honestly don't know
what keeps me tucked inside
this beautiful bubble

maybe it's healing that still beckons

or fear that i have no idea
who the new me is

or terror that i'll
make a wrong decision

or hesitation that i'll step deep
into vulnerability and sink

for now

here's to staying in the bubble
unsure of whether i'm
hiding or healing

time is weird

it's weird to hate milestones
after loving them
my whole life

you're not here
and every one you miss
makes you further
and
further
away

over it

i scream silently
no one talks
about him anymore

pain rips through me
while i smile
through gritted teeth

the unspoken american
rule is well entrenched

stay positive
don't be uncomfortable
talk about easy things

while we all die
a little inside
from silent screams

a wild teacher

some days it feels
like death is teaching
me more about love
than life ever could

knowing love can
vanish from a form
i understand
and transform into
ever present energy
and comfort
makes that love feel
indestructible
and gentle

love with the living
is terrifyingly
easy
to
miss

cruel surprises

my siblings are
on their way
to my home
so we can
enjoy a birthday
weekend together

i keep thinking
they'll surprise me
with something
or someone

my only thought is
i hope you
magically walk
through the door
with them

part of me
still hopes
this whole thing
is just a
cruel joke

a toss up

i love the days
i walk by your picture
and smile
knowing your love
goes with me today

i hate the days
i walk by your picture
knowing you're never
coming back
in familiar forms

i wish i knew
which day
would be
which

familiar

my tears feel
like home

it burns
but
it's how i
keep you
close

drop the anchor

i want to live again

to posture myself
forward into the wind
to lean curiously
toward the new
unburdened and free

yet grief and fear
anchor my body
to before times

daring me to take
a step forward
as if each step
is a betrayal
of a life i used to love
and a life i deeply miss

PART THREE

ready to live again

it's the small things

i keep thinking
i'll get better
at grief

as if it's another
self-improvement
project or
way to measure
my self-worth

i'm not getting
better at it

in case you
were wondering

i'm not as surprised
when it constantly
surprises me

we'll take that
as a win

my excuse

i remember
again
that you're gone

do i rehearse this
remembering
as a way to mark time
or as a way
to keep living inside
this familiar cave of grief?

forever

baking and dancing
in the kitchen
with my giddy heart
until i see your picture
on the fridge
and tears slice me
like a knife

you are forever
a part of every joy
and every pain

the last thing

our family ends
every call with
an *i love you*
because of you

we are determined
to know the
last thing we ever
say to each other
is the most
important
thing

wink

you winked at me today
when i needed it most
just as a big beautiful
next step emerged
from the dusty corners
of my heart after
resting for a
few years

you reminded me
this was work you
loved too

my heart flew to
meet you in the heavens

thank you

you didn't have
to do that

what a gift to still
partner with you
in this life

zip codes

how is it
that your love
feels closer
than it did
when you were
alive?

that's weird

for years
i located you
at an address
in a body
at a school
on the internet
at your job
in a text thread

now
you live
everywhere

in the trees
the birds
the water
the clouds
laughter
tears
summer trips
my breath
my ache

my joy

however love works
i'm so grateful yours
obliterated zip codes

silence hurts more

i've been the one
who forgot a
friend's loss
after a few months

assumed my friend
figured out new normals
didn't want me to
bring up sad topics
best to move on

i've been her

it's why i dig up
compassion for the
ones treating me
this way now

not talking
about him
hurts more
than talking
about him

to the one grieving —

i see how your
entire world
changed in an
instant

the others
don't see it
the ones
yet to receive
the guest
of grief

beloved
you are not
alone

we live next door
to each other
different stories
same guest

may our spirits
chat across the fence
as we
trudge and dance
this journey
together

integration

what if the goal
of grief
isn't acceptance

what if it's
integration

weaving their love
into your love
so it's an entirely
new energy

because their love
can't
actually
die

forty

i lock eyes
with the woman
in my rear view mirror

she sees my tears
i look away

we drive our
separate ways

does she wonder
why i cry?

i turn 40 today
and my brother
won't text me
won't call me
won't forget
to send a gift

i was 39
when he died

today he feels
farther away
just because
i blew out a
candle

vacation smiles

i had to delete
your photos
off my phone
to make room
for a big trip
you're supposed
to be on

yes they're backed up
but that delete
cracked my heart

again

i don't want to
make room for
new adventures
some days

i don't want to
get further away
from february

my phone fills
with new smiles

but
not
yours

swimming

we swam with
your ashes today

mom tapped a
teaspoon of you
out of a pill bottle
and we watched
your dust
sink into the lake

we jumped in
after you
shrieking with joy
at the cold refreshing
water and turtles nearby

you smiled

doing well

someone asked
how i'm doing

for the first time
in a long time i
wanted to say
i'm doing well

not a chit chat lie
or divorced from reality
all heartbreak included
i'm doing well

but what i really
wanted to say
is that i fought
through hell to
show up to every
impossible emotion
truth and fear
this season
had to offer
and i'm seeing
parts of me
i only dreamed of

for the first time
in a long time i
wanted to say
i'm doing well

so i did

closer

my heart reached
for you this morning
and you were
so
so
so
close

your words
comfort
support
interrupted
my request
mid-sentence

you met my need
before i finished
my sentence

beloved
you are closer
than i think
aren't you?

four

my grandfather's voice
cracked today
when he said
*it's always been
the four of you*

six months

it's been six months
since we talked

six months since
you texted a meme

six months since
you hugged your dog

six months since
i said goodbye to you
in that icu room

life makes zero sense
without you here

and
somehow
still

we will live
and you are here

ashes

today i received
three pounds
of your ashes

i held you in
my hands

knowing it's you
and
it's not

you live in a box
above our fireplace

and

you
live
every
where

thank you

what was he like?

that invitation is healing
the remembering is healing
speaking their name is healing

thank you to anyone who asks

what was he like?

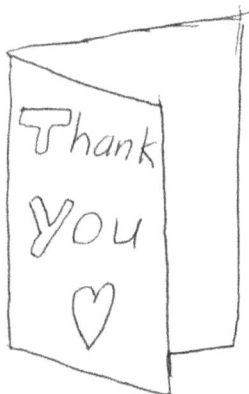

it's okay to cry

today i stood in the grocery line
hissing at my tears to stop
determined to dry them up
with sheer willpower
and embarrassment

not now
not now
not now

but why not?

maybe my tears
in that public place
would heal me

and heal another
who needs to know
it's okay to cry
in the grocery line

autumn surgery

the leaves are falling
another terrible reminder
seasons keep changing

you're still gone

i wish i could pick up
every single dying leaf
and place it back
on its tree
forcing time to
stop ticking

days

there are days
you feel so close

i know you are

then some moments
hit and the terrible
truth knocks me over
again

you died

not your love
or your energy
or your memory
or the way you love
us still

but your body
your hug
your laugh
your jokes
your smile

it died with you

some days i crumble
all over again

you died
i whisper to myself

gently reminding
my tears why they flow

discomfort

our grief
reminds people
of the fragile
powerlessness
we all wrestle

no wonder they
minimize
explain
fix and dismiss
our grief

we are a
painful reminder
of what they
can't control

when all we
need is to
be seen
believed
held

loved

begrudgingly

i can't bear the thought
of moving forward
without you here

i will

but i don't want to

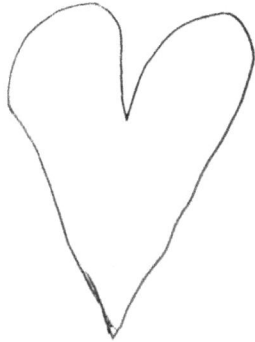

grief time

its day 206 and i keep
thinking this will hurt less

i push the to do list aside
grab a box of tissues
and sink into the couch

this cloudy monday morning
is grief time i guess

it feels good to let
tears make our decisions now

hypervigilance

i spent too much
of my life afraid
of the 2 am call
that could shatter
my world
assuming i would
die from the
terror of it all

but

i didn't die

i wish i could
trust life
more than i fear
the 2am call

mundane magic

yesterday our family
told stories of
all the places
we've taken your
ashes

state parks
the ocean in spain
my purse
a football stadium
the lake you love

may your ashes
rest and delight
in the mundane
and magic
of our lives

inheritance

your house
is under contract

a new family
will call it home

my parents said
the money you
worked so hard for
may arrive in
our bank accounts
before year's end

the dam breaks

i'm equally gutted
by your gift
and my rage
at this reality

you are beyond generous
even in death
and

i'd give up every
damn penny
for
one
more
hug

it's still valid

the high holy days of grief
arrive with noisy trumpets
and public knowing

the first week
the first month
a birthday
an anniversary

sound the bells
we lift our gaze
to name what's hidden

but what about
the quiet milestones
that no one knows
or remembers
or asks about

these hot tears on
cold september cheeks
hit differently

we honor
the quiet
milestones

— seven months

community

i sit in the last row
in a room full of
colleagues and friends

we speak of grief
frustration
overwhelm
and pain

tears land in my lap

for once
i cry in public
without fear
that i'll make another
uncomfortable

no one needs
to fix these
tears

the worst

news of a friend's loss
sends me right back
to the phone call
the shock
the nausea

rage rises that
someone i care about
will also travel
all that's about to
unfold

death is the worst

pumpkins

your ashes sit on the mantle
surrounded by fake fall leaves
and orange kid pumpkins
right under the tv that's
always got a football game on

it's your birthday month
and this season feels like you

but you're not here

we'll carve pumpkins
and play in the leaves
and blow out candles
for your birthday
and remember
again
how
much
we
miss
you

birthdays

you should be 34 today
but instead your ashes
sit on my shelf
terrible whiplash
as memories
and reality violently
collide

i don't want to
fight reality today
but every candle
and song and gift
and smile and cake
from years past
rise up unwilling
to accept it won't
happen again

so i sit here
in the early morning
hours of your birthday
feeling the tug of war
between gutting sadness
and gratitude for
the candles you got

happy birthday dear one
i'll make you a cake today
and my tears will
extinguish the flame

i don't have to
find the silver lining
today

bigger than me

the loneliness of
secret tears
can be a gift

a gift that feels
like home
because that person
was and is

home

the sharing of
secret tears
with another
reminds me
your home
is bigger
than me

maybe we don't
carry this alone

put it on the calendar

last spring
i couldn't plan
past the next month

assuming i or
someone i love
would suddenly die
because apparently
that happens now

now leaves fall
and my heart
plans something
for next spring

hearts break
then they expand

kindred spirit

the ripple approaches
my heart softly smiles
i'm at home inside her waves

the ache is familiar
never far away
no need to resist

today —
grief is a
gentle
friend

the people you love

grief pushes me
inside myself
as if i'm the
only one

then i look at the
internet on your
birthday and see
all the people
you love
doing all the
things you love

and i remember
i'm not the only one
who loves you

floating

sadness knocks me over
while i search frantically
for gratitude

find the silver lining
i implore myself
something good must
come from this horror

the gratitude is real
that i got to love
and be loved by you

but straining for gratitude
doesn't alter the course
of the wave about to
swallow me up again

so today i let go
of desperation
and i float the waves
of powerlessness
grief
anger
sadness
trusting love
can hold me
still

i want to fix it

i want to fix sadness
i want it to hurt less
i want it to get better

it does
and
it doesn't

grief keeps
reminding me
i don't have
to fix sadness

i just get
to feel it

i keep trying

some days i think
if i cry to the bottom
of whatever pain is
stuck in my chest
that it will be over

i never get there

don't take it away

you don't need to
take away my pain
for i'm learning
to hold it

but there's one
beautiful and healing
thing you can do

see me
hear me
love me

while i grieve

that's how i know
this love mattered

close

i was not prepared
for how close
you feel

is it because
i act like you are
or because
you're actually
as close as my
next breath?

because you
feel *that* close

when i'm confused
and scared
or laughing
and relaxed
you enter
my mind
and
you're
right
there

i had no idea
death could
feel like this

— grateful

joyful disaster

the last post
my brother liked
on my feed was
a picture of my
smiling son and
the words
my heart
is so happy

i love that
this is the last
post he saw

and —
i hate this

some days
it makes me
feel like my
joy will invite
another disaster

our last hug

a year ago
you hugged me
for the last time

your strong arms
held me for
a moment
an *i love you*
a *good to see you*

not knowing it
wasn't just
about that week
it was everything

you held me in life
in a way i rarely
knew i needed

your nods and
support made
me think i could fly

your love showed
me worlds beyond
myself

we didn't know
it was the last one
otherwise
i would have
never let go

tug of war

my memories
and reality
love to argue

cozy thoughts
of holiday parades
late night games
crescent rolls
and fudge
fight for top
billing while
my body
freezes in grief

he's not here
my body whispers

all while my memories
keep creating the
holiday we've long loved

— confusion

the night before thanksgiving

it's the night before
thanksgiving
and you're not
on the couch
with pizza rolls
and your phone
watching a movie
with the guys

instead we all
went to bed early
and the living room
is empty
lit by a few
twinkle lights
and grief

we yawn
from long travel days
but maybe we're
more tired from
finally arriving
at this terrible place

the first major holiday
without you

so tonight
we've brushed our teeth
cracked jokes in the hallway
and lie in our beds
glad to be together again

heartbroken that
you're not here
in body

even though we
know your spirit
laughed at the names
we made up on that game
rolled your eyes when
we told a story about you
smiled when your nephew
proudly filled his dinner roll
with jelly and proclaimed
himself just like jeremy

maybe that's why
it's hard

you're here
and
you're
not

summoning the wave

sometimes i summon
the wave of grief
to visit my shores
thinking that will
stop the waves from
hitting when i'm
not ready

it never works

marking time

each day i cross
off another
box on the calendar
pretending i'm marking
dance practices
flu shots
meetings
but secretly
each line pushes
me closer to the moment
the unspoken expectations
whisper about

one year

somewhere i picked up
that i'm supposed to
be magically over this
by then

i won't be
and i've decided
that's okay

surprise

some days i think
new memories
will erase you
as if my brain
can only hold
one set of stories
at a time

but it's wild
how making new
memories in the places
you've been

heals

ornament

i hate that your face
is on my christmas tree

a place reserved for
growing kids
and those long gone

ornaments honor
the past
and i hate that
you've joined
the past

you should be
present
future
and later
today

costco cheese

in grief we birth
something new

a life without them
a life that continues on
in new form

the labor hurts
as muscles contract
push
relax
and push
again

the pain has a purpose

it delivers us
into our new life

sometimes the
water breaks in the
cheese aisle at costco
while staring at the ground
wiping the tears away

compass

when life is upside down
grief is now
a compass
so familiar
so steady

the place that
breathes me home

one might say
i should move on
but isn't grief
just another name
for love?

this grief
and this love
are
my
center

the end is coming

writing these poems
gave me structure
and purpose when
grief crashed
my world

as i near the end
of this body of work
i feel grief shoving
me into a rhythmless
void

part of me wants
to crawl back
inside these words
as if they give
permission to grieve
without falling
all the way apart

another part of me
that's stronger
than i realize
knows how to ride
these waves

she knows i'll fall
and that i'll be okay

but maybe worst of all —
this project coming to an end
makes me realize

i have
to start
living
again

and that
maybe

i want to

annoying

sometimes
when joy
floods my heart
grief shoves the
door open
demanding
an invite to the party

i sigh

and welcome
grief
in
too

holy tears

sometimes i avoid the tears
as if they'll pull me down
into oblivion

sometimes i consider it an honor
to cry for the beloved i lost

these tears are holy
sacred
beautiful

they tell a story of love so deep
it will take a lifetime of tears
to tell it well

holiday grief

i tried to christmas

we got the gifts and made the cookies
we made the menu and bought the food
we scheduled the video calls and texted friends
we read the story and embodied gratitude

but somewhere between late morning
and early afternoon
my body sent an unmistakable message

i'm sad
today is heavy
this is hard

so i stepped away a few times
to cry and listen to my body
after years of ignoring her
she makes my decisions now

but my body couldn't reconcile
my effort with reality

layers of grief live in my body
they don't care what the calendar says
so i finally gave in for good

today is a sad christmas
and i think that's okay

here's to football and naps
puzzles and tears

pizza instead of the fancy menu
bedtime stories and deep sighs
december rain on the skylight and soft blankets

we release all expectations
and the ridiculous game of
matching memories from
years long past

we breathe deeply of *this* moment
in all its complexity

love is still here
and i think she loves it
when we receive it as our actual self
not the one we think we're supposed to be today

thank god

secret videos

there's a video
on my phone of
my mom walking
beside my brother's
hospital bed
at 4:00 am
while he's pushed
into surgery to
save someone
else's life

hospital staff
line the hallways
and clap

they call it an
honor walk

they clap for
his generosity
his life
his broken mother
gripping the arm rail
soaking in the
last few moments
with her baby's body

they clap because
death turns into life
over and over
over and over

the heartbreaking parade
pauses at the elevator
signaling to my mom
it's time to say goodbye

they bless his body
with gratitude and love

they press the button
doors open
and my brother
is wheeled out of view

my mom loves him
from beginning to end
and beyond

this video is ours
to remember
life turns into death
into life into death
with terror and grace

we honor it all

all this love

what will we do
with the love
of our beloved
that lives in us?

some days
we hold it tight
cradling the exact experience
it gave us
devastated it's gone
in a way we understood

but what if other days
we know love
is the whole point
of this life

to pass on
what changed us

to offer as gift
what loved us

to love as
we've been loved

maybe we get
to do both

we hold them close
while we give their love away

because
it actually
can't die

love only multiplies

radical acceptance

wise people say
radical acceptance
is a healing and hard practice

i can't bring you back

if i'm more honest
than i want to be
part of me believed
writing this book
would bring you back

that maybe i could save you
with words and love

look, world
i cried enough
i grieved enough
i did what you told me to do
where is he?

i threw stones into
the ocean today
each one full of
rage and powerlessness

you're not coming back

part of me knows it's true
part of me will try to outrun it
forever

my therapist says
part of our heart
never fully accepts death

the love is too strong

— i think i'm okay with that

calendar thieves

the new year
usually holds
such possibility
and wonder

now i know
life could be
stolen again
this year

it feels foolish
to look for joy
this january one

but i will
even if
i'm scared

a toss up

i love the days
i walk by your picture
and smile
knowing your love
goes with me today

i hate the days
i walk by your picture
and pain rips through me
knowing you're never
coming back
in familiar form

i wish i knew
which day
would be
which

death is weird

someone asked
what's been the biggest
surprise on this grief journey

i thought about it
and said

love is weird
so is death

i talk to him
all the time
he feels close
involved
present

my love for him
has only grown

turns out love can't die

he's
still
here

this good

someone told me
the other day that
your love is still
healing our family

that your death
broke us open
and we drew
closer
instead
of farther away

it's true

your love
is a resounding
chord underneath
our lives
inviting us into
healing and grace
love and wisdom

how are you
this good to us

still?

love is everywhere

beloved —

i wish
you
were
here

i am

relief

the best thing
someone told me

you never have
to get over this

— grief

jeremy's story

I'm a writer. I love putting words together to paint a new perspective or story. It's magic and love when these words then meet truth in you. I adore the power of words.

But I hate this sentence: My brother died five weeks ago.

Maybe if I write it a million times, my brain will believe it's true. The shock is real.

On Friday, February 18, 2022, my husband and I said goodbye to our kids and my mom and flew to Los Angeles for a long-awaited 40th birthday trip with our college friends. We landed at LAX and I loved seeing all the LA Rams gear following their Super Bowl win earlier that week. I said to Aaron, "Let's look this weekend for a great Rams shirt for Jeremy. He'd love it!"

Our friends picked us up and we enjoyed lunch by the beach as we drove to a hotel for the night. We got dressed up and walked to the theater nearby to see Wicked. Anxiety descended as the show started and I ended up watching the first half from the lobby. Sitting high up in theaters has long been an anxiety trigger for me so I didn't think much of it.

The second half began and I headed into the theater to try to enjoy the show.

I had no idea that, as I watched the second half, my youngest brother, Jeremy, experienced a brain bleed while driving. Two people were following him on the road and saw him driving normally up O'Malley Road in Anchorage, Alaska. Then they saw him start to drive erratically. He crossed into oncoming traffic and over snow berms. They called 911 and followed his car until Jeremy's vehicle ended up in a snowbank, narrowly missing a fire hydrant. A doctor and nurse, they jumped out of their car to get to Jeremy. Jeremy was able to talk and answer a couple questions. Then it was clear he was not okay. Others who stopped to help wrapped him in a blanket and helped him lie down on the cold Alaskan sidewalk. They prayed with him and talked with him until medics arrived. My brother wasn't alone in his last moments.

We later learned Jeremy experienced an AVM (arteriovenous malformation) that he likely had since birth. It's not genetic. Some survive a rupture depending on where it's located. Jeremy's AVM was nestled deep in the back of his brain and medical professionals did everything they could, especially since he was so young, but his body didn't respond. His heart and organs continued to function but his brain died.

My brother was less than a mile from his home. If he'd gotten home, he would have died alone. Instead, the medical professionals got Jeremy to the hospital and machines kept him technically alive until our family could get there.

The hospital started calling our family in the middle of the night. My other brother, Ryan, and his girlfriend at the time, Emily, were in Italy when he got the call. My mom was at my house in Washington with our kids. My dad was in Oregon at home. My sister was in Oregon at home. I missed the call from the hospital while I was sleeping at the hotel in California. My husband heard a call come in at 4:45 am. I saw the missed calls and called the hospital. They said it was about my brother and the prognosis was not good. I immediately called my mom and she shared what she knew.

―――――

How can I describe that moment?

My stomach dropped. My entire body went into fight or flight mode. I dragged my shaky self to the bathroom for a minute. I sat down on the hotel bed with my husband. I cried. I mindlessly started picking up my things and putting them in my luggage. We booked a flight back to Seattle. I called my brother. I texted my sister.

At the airport, I walked by the same shirt I'd seen the day before. I bought it and tucked it in my bag. I stared out the window for two hours as we flew home. I talked to Jeremy. I cried with him. I told him it was okay to let go if he needed to. I told him how much we loved him.

It became obvious over the next day or so that Jeremy wouldn't survive this. Our goal was to get the family there to say goodbye. I'll never forget standing near the escalator in the N concourse at SeaTac and seeing Ryan running toward me. This

guy had just flown around the world for a day and a half so he could say goodbye to his best friend. His person. We clung to each other and sobbed.

We got off our plane in Anchorage and drove to the hospital. I walked into the same place where I gave birth to my daughter. The same place where I later rushed her in as she experienced a life-threatening allergic reaction. Now, I fumbled my way through some Covid questions and rode the elevator up to ICU with my sister. Ryan, his girlfriend, Emily, and I walked into the waiting room and hugged my parents.

As someone with terrible hospital anxiety, this was my worst nightmare. I took a deep breath and walked back to Jeremy's room with my sister and mom. I rounded the corner and my breath hitched. There he was. Sitting up in bed with his eyes closed. Breathing normally and hooked up to machines. Almost as if he'd open his eyes and smile.

I sat on a chair next to the bed and anxiously talked to him. I told him how much I loved him. How much he meant to so many people. I cried. At one point, I looked up and a tear rolled down his cheek. It took my breath away. I looked over at my mom and sister. Mom reminded us they put gel on his eyelids to keep them closed. Intellectually I knew it wasn't a sign of emotion from my little brother. But my heart exploded. It felt like he was with me for a second. That our entire life of love was wrapped up in that one tear.

The next few days were a blur. People brought us food, mattresses, airline miles, gift cards. The doctors ran every test they could think of to ensure there wasn't anything else that could be done. We knew he was gone. We flew up the rest of our families and started planning a service for the following Saturday.

On Monday at 4:00 pm Alaska time, they gave the official death pronouncement. Then his care was transferred to the organ donation team. Jeremy had chosen to have his organs donated if that was ever needed and because people got him to the hospital so quickly, he was able to share many of his organs with families desperately waiting for their miracle.

That Friday, we gathered at the flagpole at Providence Medical Center to help raise a flag in honor of Jeremy's gift of life. Jeremy's dear friends, Easter, Sam and their family sang. Jeremy's beloved dog, Kodos, howled a song Jeremy taught him. I read Jeremy's obituary, we raised the donor flag and prayed together.

On Saturday, we gathered at St. John United Methodist Church, our family's home church, to grieve and honor Jeremy's life. It was full of tears, story, laughter, and truth. Jeremy's beloved friends toasted him with 5 hour energy shots and four pastors eulogized him. My parents, siblings, and Emily shared. A dear friend read scripture in Jeremy's sloth costume, and the four nieces and nephews put some of Jeremy's favorite things on the altar. We invited people to wear Hawaiian shirts in honor of Jeremy's love of the state and his overall chill vibe.

A while back, Jeremy told friends he wanted a bounce house at his funeral so a friend made it happen. I'll never forget walking out of the packed sanctuary and into the bounce house. Feeling some joy at that moment was a gift straight from Jeremy's heart. A tiny crack of this horrific heartbreak healed as we jumped and laughed. On the hardest day of our lives, he gave us laughter.

Looking back, we each had a good phone call with Jeremy in the last few days of his life. And just about all those calls ended with, "Love you, Jeremy. Love you too."

He knew how much we loved him. I'm so damn grateful he knew.

Friends, may I be another voice in your corner gently reminding you it could all be over in an instant. Love your people. Apologize. Make things right. Make the memory. One day you may be taking screenshots of everything that person ever said to you.

So, there you go. A bit of what happened in the past five weeks.

———

I'm a writer, through and through. My phone is full of notes and poems. I'm a full-time noticer of life and wildly curious about how we show up to whatever falls into our hands.

Not a single part of me wants to show up to this story. I am devastated. And yet, I will. I have to.

Honestly, I've spent most of my life wracked with anxiety, trying to make sure moments like this never happened. But again I learn, we can't control this life as much as we'd like. I've seen how resilient our bodies are. I got the worst news of my life and my body kept breathing. We fall apart. We cry. We ache. We call. We plan. But we keep breathing.

Within hours of the terrible news, I started writing. Putting my feelings into words helped me feel them. I was surprised how quickly the words came, almost with an unstoppable force. I will continue writing as the words arrive.

Losing my brother only three weeks after a life-changing career shift is a lot to process. I will continue to do the thing I know to do: show up, pay attention, cooperate with God, release the outcome.

Because the work and invitations glimmering on the horizon stir my soul to life. I'm taking Jeremy's love with me as I ever so gently move that direction.

Here's to the love we carry from our beloveds.

Here's to the pain we must feel and name.

Here's to the lives we still get to live.

Thank you, dear reader, for bearing witness to this part of my story. It's healing to share it. Thank you for receiving it.

May we hold all our lives with open hands, trusting the One who guides us still.

Palms up.

funeral

Someone said sadness is the soul's way of knowing something mattered. Jeremy mattered.

He was my baby brother. He was your son, your brother, your friend, your encourager, your roommate, your co-worker, someone you admired from a distance. An acquaintance who made you laugh. And if you knew Jeremy, you probably knew Kodos. They're a package deal. Kodos is enjoying lots of extra love and treats this week. But he's also looking out the window for Jeremy to come running up the stairs to say hi.

I took an early morning walk on the icy sidewalks up to our old house this week. I stood outside the house and felt it pulse with memory and love. I saw the deck where we gathered to celebrate graduations and birthdays. I saw the living room where we opened Christmas gifts and played with my daughter. I saw the basement where he played video games with the guys.

As the pink sunrise started to dance on the horizon, I stood outside our childhood home and wept in the cold air.

I felt his presence everywhere. I asked Jeremy what he wanted people to know.

I felt him say: "Tell them how much I love them. I'm still here. My love is here.

Tell them that they are made of love."

Ready or not, we are just beginning to imagine a world without Jeremy's presence. But we never have to imagine a world without Jeremy's love. That's our job now. To love like he did.

A night or two ago I FaceTimed my kids. There was laughter and giggling and I felt my heart soar for a moment. The joy felt deeper than before. Then the tears came. A little survivor guilt that I was laughing in the midst of such deep loss.

But I caught myself and understood again that deep pain and deep love go together. Jeremy would want all this love we shared to translate into more love and joy. More adventures. More generosity.

And. I think he'd understand the tears too. He'd give us a hug today because he gets it. We miss him. We love him.

I leave you with some beautiful words Jeremy wrote in his phone. May it be true for us all. He wrote:

> *I am God's creation.*
> *I am loved.*
> *I am the decider of my reactions.*
> *God is forgiving.*
> *God is all knowing and loving.*
> *God is always with me.*

Jeremy, we loved loving you and being loved by you. Thank you for sharing your life so generously with us. This hurts so terribly because there was so much love.

Love you brother. I'll be one of your big sisters forever.

for a grieving mother

today you sit in the shattered shards
of your son's life
a life you birthed
a life you labored
a life you held
a life you nurtured

you loved him beautifully
provided all he needed
loved him when he felt lonely
reminded him who he was when he forgot
expanded his world
embodied a safe place for him to land

then you watched him look beyond
all you gave him
wondering what this life could be
what he could do
who he could love
what he could see

he looked back at you
seeking your permission
your blessing
your love

you took a deep breath
softly smiled
and gently nodded
he smiled back
and soared into his new life

all you gave him held him
through every moment

then you got the call
you rushed to his side
held him
spoke to him
cried with him
loved him

the end arrived both softly
and with the force of a freight train

you did all you knew to do
you labored this beautiful soul
into his next life
with the same love
you labored him into
this life

he knew your love to the end
he knows your love still

he's looking back at you

seeking your permission
your blessing
your love

you take a deep breath
softly smile
and gently nod
he smiles back
and soars into his new life

for a grieving father

today you exist inside an ache
you've never known before

the loss of a son
a human you loved
nurtured
supported
helped create

now you look around
at a life that makes little sense
without him here

the quiet is both comforting
and deeply painful

for 33 years
this son was a call away
to talk about the game
work

life
plans
love

the wounded places you carry
found deep grace in this child
he saw your heart
knew what could be
believed in new realities
new healing

now you see this same love
resurrecting in your other son
and it astounds you

could it be that this gospel we love
is more true than we ever imagined?

could it be true for us all?

that no pain is too deep to be healed
that we could step into new life still

as you journey forward with his love
to guide you
may his grace forgive any lingering regrets
may his patience deepen the moment
may his humor make you smile
may his adventure send you out
may his love of family bring you home
may his generosity inspire yours
may his memory feel like a long hug

may your last conversation and last

"i love you's" remind you forever
that this life with your son mattered
that he's with you
right here
forever

for a grieving brother

today you stand in a whole new life
a life you never asked for
a life you never imagined

a life without the physical presence of
your brother

for 33 years, you protected him
laughed with him
argued with him
played with him
adventured with him

he was a constant loyal force
that grounded your life

his love steadied you
when nothing else made sense

now you stand on new ground
holding both this aching loss

and a new lease on life

your brain and heart beat
with new life

both yours and his

as you step forward into this brave new life
may the deep unending love of your brother
go before you

may he comfort you in the tears
may he roll his eyes when you joke
may he raise a glass when you celebrate
may he wink when you need it
may he soar with you as you travel

may his love infuse your best relationships
may his generosity guide your choices
may his patience quiet your heart
may his hope point you toward the new
may his joy dance in your body

because this beloved is part of you
you cannot leave him
and he cannot leave you

you get to bravely open your hands
every day to receive him
and you'll have all you need

for a grieving sister

nineteen months separated
you and your brother

the kid who looked up to you
adored you
loved you

and with one phone call
he was gone

the bottom fell out of this life
we thought was safe
predictable
known
planned

now we sit in the brokenness
hearts shattered
bodies exhausted
feeling it all
and hating it all

the annoying part of this blessing
is that you so well know
what he'd want you to do next

he'd see the tears and give you a hug
he'd see your attempt to get through the day
and he'd pour you a drink
he'd see the challenges and he'd listen
he'd see the brave steps into new life and he'd cheer you on
he'd raise a glass to the trips you plan
he'd nod when you're uncertain
he'd tease you when you need it
he'd pick up your kids and make them giggle
he'd hang with your husband and they'd laugh
he'd see the hardest part of this is losing him
and he gets it — he misses you too

may you feel the best and most beautiful
parts of your brother
all day every day

his love beats in your heart
his courage courses through your veins
his adventure invites you forward
his generosity guides you always

he's here with you — forever

for grieving nieces + nephews

there once were four cousins
who loved their uncle jeremy
so much

he made them laugh
he played with them
he sent gifts and love
he listened to their stories

then one day something happened
and he was gone

these beloved kids
wouldn't see their uncle jeremy
in the same way anymore

they felt sad and confused
as adults cried and life continued

they played soccer and went to school

they watched a show and played games
yet the sadness surprised them sometimes

then one day they felt uncle jeremy's love
whispering to them and he said,

i miss you
i love you
my love is here with you

whenever you see a
sunrise or sunset
a butterfly or your favorite bird
your parents hugging or family laughing
i am here with you

whenever you feel love
i am here with you

when you're proud of yourself
or confused and worried
i am here with you

when you miss me
know i'm missing you too

so my beloveds
may you know
deep in your heart
that uncle jeremy
is always with you
when you laugh
play
adventure
try something new

feel scared or sad

talk to him anytime
and he's right here with you

telling you again,
"i love you forever!"

kidneys

I never thought I'd write a letter to the recipients of my brother's kidneys. Or get a letter in return.

But, well. Here we are.

————

My name is Jenny and I'm so very grateful my brother's kidney is changing your life. Jeremy is my little brother and was in his 30s. He's part of a big and beautiful family that loved him deeply. Jeremy has two sisters and a brother, a mom and dad, two brothers-in-law, and four nieces and nephews.

One thing you should know about Jeremy is how generous of a guy he was. He was the first to buy someone's meal or a plane ticket or plan a big trip. Jeremy loved his friends and they made great memories together. He loved his dog, Kodos, with everything inside him. Jeremy loved living in Alaska.

Knowing Jeremy, he'd be really excited you get a new lease on life. He'd be cheering you on. His love is really big and we sense him here with us still. Our family is honored to have part of him living inside you. May you go forth and live with abundance and joy. It's the best way we can honor what mattered so much to him.

———

The recipient, T. (36 yo) has had type one diabetes for 23 years and been on dialysis for 10 years. She was diagnosed with kidney failure after the birth of a son. T. lost her eyesight after a stroke. She writes, "I am so grateful for your family for giving me this opportunity of a new life; not only for me but for my son."

Another recipient, A. was diagnosed with an incurable kidney disease 12 years ago during a pregnancy and has been on dialysis since that time. "Your loved one will always be a part of me and for that I will be forever grateful. Thank you for entrusting me with a living legacy from your loved one."

from my children

the saddest moment of my life
by wesley smith
8 years old

i look up at the stars
as i say goodbye
to someone i will
never see again

his love was here
and it still is

i will see him again
just in a different way

Isabella (11 years old) enjoyed washing cars with her Uncle Jeremy

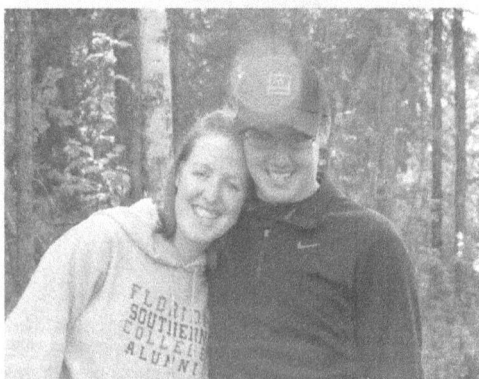

acknowledgments

St. John United Methodist Church family - I'll never forget the early weeks when you scooped up our family and held us with food, air miles, cars, hugs, beds, notes, and more food. You are love embodied.

Andy, Emily, Autumn & Nico - I know Jeremy *loves* that it took four pastor friends to eulogize him. Thank you for loving him and letting him see the human inside the pastoral role. He loved you.

Deb - You were one of my first phone calls when life went upside down. Thank you for telling me from day one that it's okay to feel it all. You knew I'd try to live in my head. My body thanks you.

Debbie - Our virtual therapy sessions gave me (and my family) a touchpoint that it was all normal and awful and we would get through the early months.

Janelle, Tanya, Erynne, Risa, April B, Amy A, April C, Amy F - Your texts and calls in the first year reminded me I still existed. Thank you for loving me so well.

Lara - We reconnected just when I needed it. You sat with me in coffee shops and asked to hear stories of him. I knew the loss of your beloved dad shaped your love for this part of my journey and it felt like holy ground. What joy to grieve and heal together.

Erin - You brought me Mexican food and never tried to fix the grief. You were one of the first to receive this manuscript and your edits created more love for our readers. Big big big love.

Kate - You listened and responded to every single Marco Polo message this year as I stumbled through grief. Your arms held it all. Thank you forever.

Ryan & Lauren - Figuring out how to be the new power block has been both painful and beautiful. Jeremy draws us together in a way I love. We joke that he'd hardly recognize us now. I'm glad his love is still here, bringing so much beauty out of each of us. I'll always wish it was still the four of us though.

Mom & Dad - You could have hidden your grief and denied our family the healing we needed but you didn't. You opened your arms wide to whatever emerged from this excruciating year. Who would have guessed it'd be our deepest healing yet. Love you forever.

Isabella & Wesley - It must have been weird to see your mom feel so sad this year. Your hugs and understanding let me be a grieving sister when I needed it most. Sharing this grief journey with you is teaching us that love really never dies. May this guide us always.

Aaron - Thank you for holding my hand through this ridiculous year. For making dinner so I could crawl into bed early. For loving our kids when I felt like a zombie. For listening to stories that turned to tears. For sharing your love of our brother. I'm forever grateful you got to love him and be loved by him for twenty years.

Jeremy - I keep thinking I should refer to you in the past tense. But then I feel your presence and love wash through and the truth remains — you're still here. Thank you for sitting with me as each of these poems came to life. It was the honor of my life to co-create these with you. May your love keep welcoming people home to themselves and the one life we get to live.

Thank you for loving us still.

about the author

In a time when it's harder than ever to look reality in the eye, Jenny Smith offers people the courage to show up authentically to all of life's complexities. As a writer and speaker, Jenny teaches that we cultivate resilience and healing when we move from the story of fear and avoidance toward a posture of curiosity and trust. Drawing on her own life experience, Jenny treats sensitive topics like mental health, burnout, spirituality, neurodivergence, and grief with disarming humor and grace, offering hope that the way to wholeness is often right through the heart of the hard things. Connect at jennysmithwrites.com.

facebook.com/jennysmithwrites
instagram.com/jennysmithwrites
tiktok.com/@jennysmithwrites

www.ingramcontent.com/pod-product-compliance
Lightning Source LLC
Chambersburg PA
CBHW051418090426
42737CB00014B/2728